World Book, Inc.
180 North LaSalle Street
Suite 900
Chicago, Illinois 60601
USA

For information about other "True or False?" titles, as well as other World Book print and digital publications, please go to www.worldbook.com.

For information about other World Book publications, call 1-800-WORLDBK (967-5325).

For information about sales to schools and libraries, call 1-800-975-3250 (United States) or 1-800-837-5365 (Canada).

Library of Congress Cataloging-in-Publication Data for this volume has been applied for.

True or False?
ISBN: 978-0-7166-3725-7 (set, hc.)

Pirates
ISBN: 978-0-7166-3731-8 (hc.)

Also available as:
ISBN: 978-0-7166-3741-7 (e-book)

Printed in China by Shenzhen Wing King Tong Paper Products Co., Ltd., Shenzhen, Guangdong
1st printing July 2018

Staff

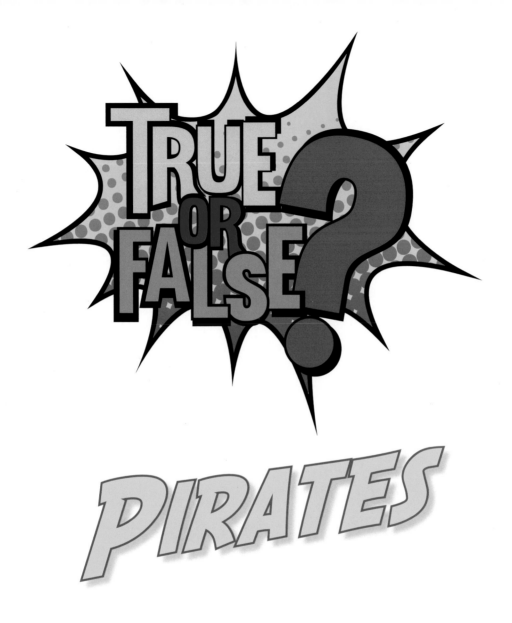

PIRATES

WORLD
BOOK

www.worldbook.com

TRUE OR FALSE?

**Pirates only exist
in movies and books.**

FALSE!

Pirates have been around for as long as there have been ships. A pirate is someone who captures ships and takes their cargo. Many famous pirates raided ships sailing in the Caribbean Sea in the late 1600's and early 1700's.

The 1600's and early 1700's have been called the Golden Age of Piracy.

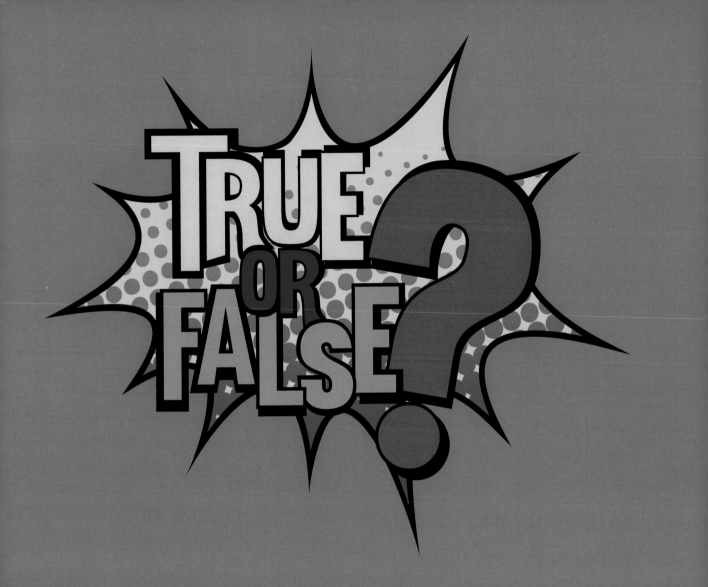

TRUE OR FALSE?

Pirates delighted
in killing their prisoners.

9

Pirates usually tried to avoid killing people. Boat crews were more likely to give up without a fight if they knew their lives would be spared.

Also, prisoners could be just as valuable as loot. They could be freed in exchange for money, called ransom, or even sold into slavery.

TRUE OR FALSE?

The famous pirate flag, with a skull and two crossed bones, is known as the Jolly Roger.

The flag is called the Jolly Roger.
But nobody knows exactly why.

Some people think it comes from "Old Jolly," a nickname for the Devil.

Many pirates were women. One of the most famous was an Irish captain named Grace O'Malley. Her ships sailed along the coasts of Ireland and Scotland in the 1500's.

19

The crew of a pirate ship had to obey its captain without question.

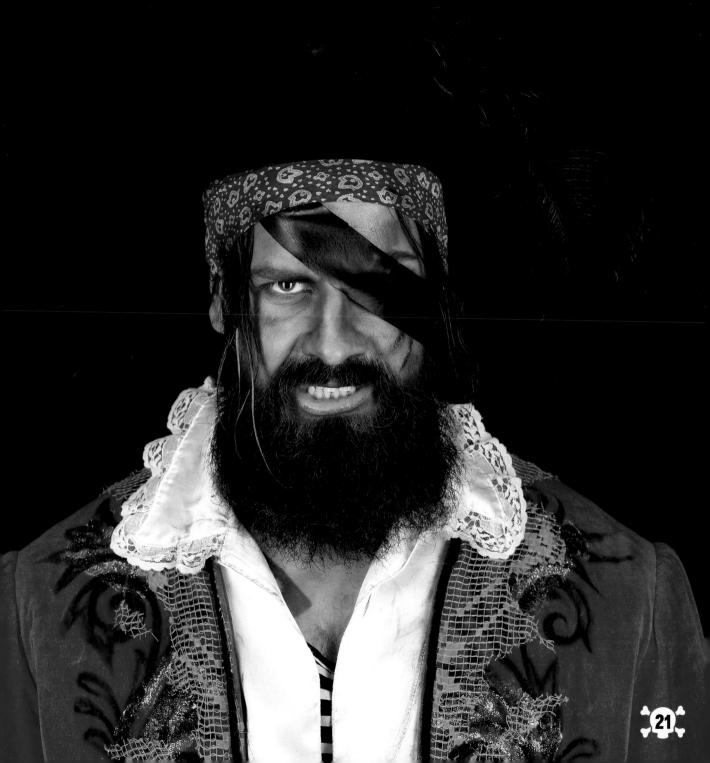

FALSE!

Pirate crews often voted on important decisions. The crew had a say in where to go, what ships to raid, and what to do with prisoners.

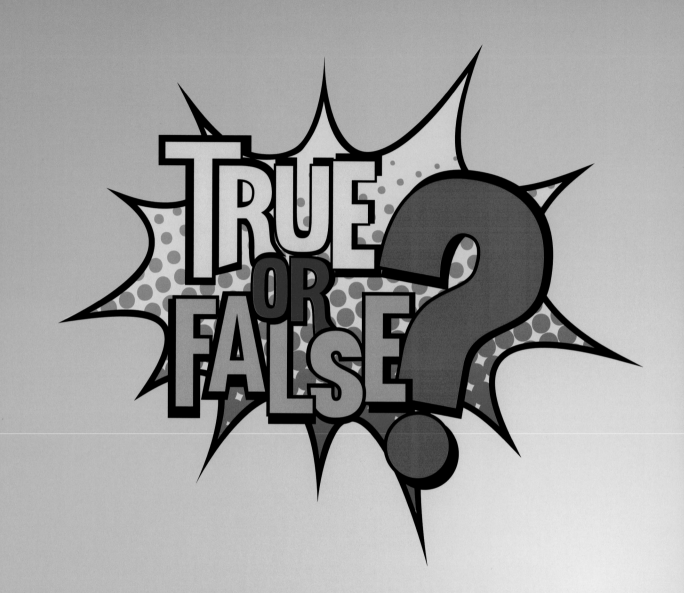

The benefits of a being a pirate included insurance.

Most pirate ships were run according to a contract (written agreement). Among other things, the contract called for crew members to be paid for any injuries they received.

One of the most feared pirates,
Edward Teach, was known
by his nickname, the Teacher.

Teach was known by the nickname
Blackbeard. Some people say Blackbeard
set pieces of twisted paper and cloth on fire
and stuck them in his hat. The pirate hoped
the smoke would frighten his enemies,
making them think he was a demon.

All pirates were outlaws.

Some kings and queens gave sea captains special papers called letters of mark. The papers made it legal for these captains to attack the ships of other nations. These "legal" pirates were called privateers.

TRUE OR FALSE?

Two of the most famous pirates —
Captain Hook and Long John Silver —
were not even real.

Captain Hook is the villain of the story of *Peter Pan,* by J. M. Barrie. Long John Silver is the main villain in the novel *Treasure Island,* by Robert Louis Stevenson.

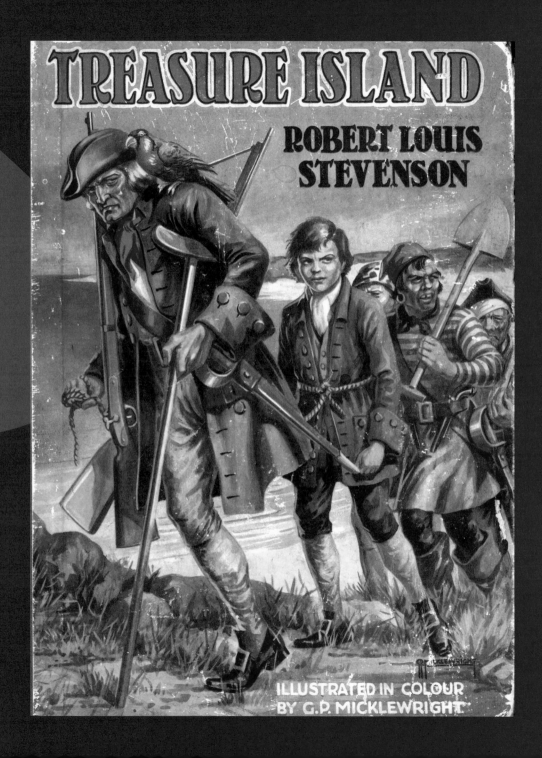

TREASURE ISLAND

ROBERT LOUIS STEVENSON

ILLUSTRATED IN COLOUR
BY G.P. MICKLEWRIGHT

Calico Jack was the only cat
to ever captain a pirate ship.

Calico Jack is the nickname of
John Rackham, a famous human pirate
of the early 1700's. He wore clothing
made from a cheap cloth called calico.

TRUE OR FALSE?

The last pirates died
hundreds of years ago.

Piracy still happens today. Modern pirates use small, fast boats and heavy weapons to capture ships and kidnap crews. Piracy is no laughing matter. Millions of dollars are lost to pirates every year.

To improve their eyesight,
some pirates pierced their ears.

49

50

Pirates believed in some strange things — called superstitions — like most people living in the 1600's and1700's did. One superstition some pirates believed was that wearing a gold earring would help them see better.

TRUE OR FALSE?

People did not think piracy was a bad crime. If they were caught, pirates might have gone to jail for a time, and they had to give back their loot.

People have always thought that piracy is a terrible crime. Many pirates who were caught were hanged to death.

The most successful pirate ever was a Chinese woman.

57

A woman named Ching Shih terrorized ships in the China Sea in the early 1800's. She commanded hundreds of boats and thousands of pirates.

TRUE OR FALSE?

Pirates today try to trap ships by sending them fake e-mails. This crime is called internet piracy.

Internet piracy is copying and sharing computer files that you do not own or have permission to share. Internet pirates share movies, music, and video games without paying for them. Internet piracy is a crime.

Letters   Data

Movies   Music   Photos

Games   Videos   Fil

63

TRUE OR FALSE?

Pirates were unhappy people who lived hard, unpleasant lives.

FALSE!

Many sailors became pirates because they got more money as pirates. Pirate ships usually were better than navy or merchant ships.

Saying "arrrgh" and "yo, ho, ho" is the thing to do on International Talk Like a Pirate Day.

The day was thought up by a couple of friends and made popular by the American humorist Dave Barry. Talk Like a Pirate Day is celebrated on September 19. On that day, impress your friends with some pirate phrases.

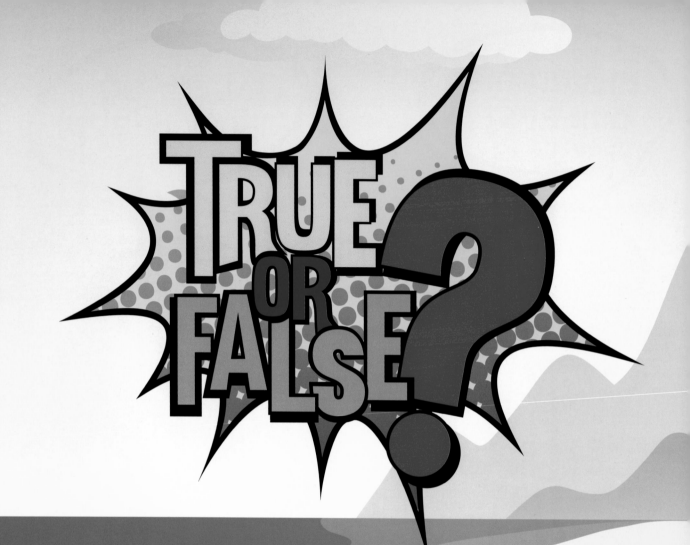

TRUE OR FALSE?

The pirate captain David Jones kept all his treasure in a well-locked box. This box became known as Davy Jones's Locker.

FALSE!

When pirates say "Davy Jones's Locker," they really mean the bottom of the sea. Davy Jones was a name sailors used for the Devil. When ships sink, they end up in Davy Jones's Locker.

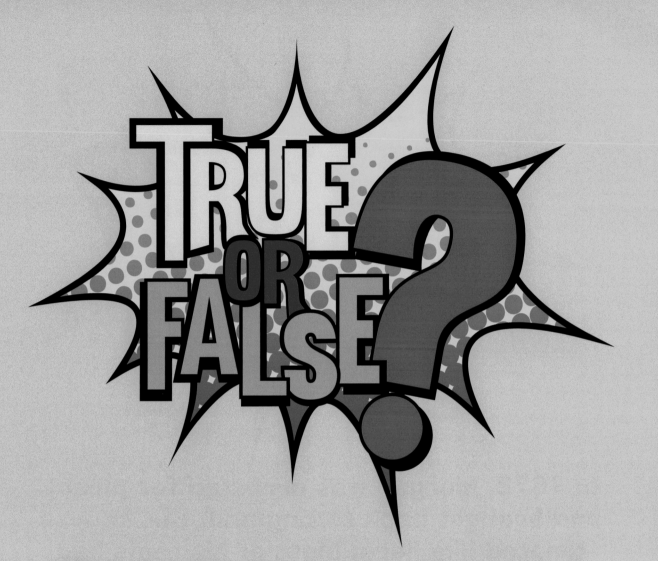

After he was arrested on the island of Jamaica, the pirate captain Henry Morgan was sent to England. He was tried and hanged there for his piratical ways.

In 1672, Morgan was arrested for piracy and brought back to England. But he was treated like hero. Most of his raids had been on the ships and colonies of Spain, England's enemy at the time. The English even gave Morgan an important government job in Jamaica.

The pirate captain Bartolomeu Portugues made a daring escape from a Spanish ship, even though he did not know how to swim.

Portugues was a prisoner on a Spanish ship. He got around his guards and climbed overboard. He could not swim, so he used empty wine bottles to help him float to shore. The daring Portugues later captured the same ship!

Pirates often buried their treasure.

Many pirate stories tell of buried treasure.
Most pirates enjoyed their money, rather
than saving it in a hole on a beach. They
spent their coin on food, drink, and fun.

There was once an entire
city run by pirates.

In the early 1700's, pirates took over the city of Nassau, in the group of islands called the Bahamas. Nassau became a "pirate republic," a place where pirates were in charge!

"Citizens" of this republic included some of the most famous historical pirates: Charles Vane, Benjamin Hornigold, Calico Jack Rackham, Anne Bonny, Mary Read, and Edward Teach, known as Blackbeard.

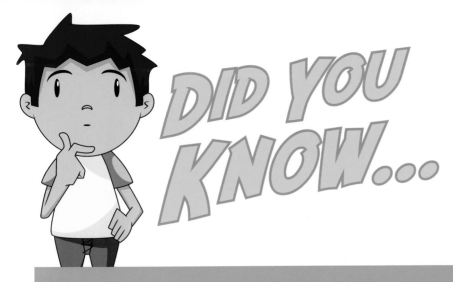

DID YOU KNOW...

Our modern ideas about the **way pirates talk** don't come from history. They mostly come from the film *Treasure Island* (1950).

Pirates called the **Barbary Corsairs** raided the Mediterranean Sea from the **1500's to the early 1800's.**

Pirates sometimes **used ropes** to drag a victim beneath their boat, a punishment called keelhauling.

Scholars think **pirates wore eyepatches** to preserve night vision in one eye, helping them to see in the shadows below decks.

In 1996, divers **found the wreck** of Blackbeard's ship, the *Queen Anne's Revenge,* in North Carolina, in the United States.

As a young man, the Roman general Julius Caesar was **captured by pirates.**

There are no historical records **of pirates carrying parrots** on their shoulders.

Index

Acknowledgments

Cover: © Dta93/Shutterstock; © Glenda/Shutterstock; © Ded Mazay, Shutterstock

4   From *Pirates of the Caribbean: On Stranger Tides* (© Walt Disney Pictures)

7   *A Customs Brig Engaging the Pirate Lugger 'Will Watch'* (19th century), oil on canvas by Francis Hustwick; Private Collection/© Calvados Art Ltd. (Bridgeman Images)

8-27   © Shutterstock

29-30   © Photo Researchers/Alamy Images

33   *Bartholemy and his men were all ready for their hot and bloody work* (20th century), colour lithograph by George Alfred Williams; Private Collection/© Look and Learn (Bridgeman Images)

35   *Pirates on the Island of Tortuga* (20th century), colour lithograph by George Alfred Williams; Private Collection/© Look and Learn (Bridgeman Images)

36   From *Peter Pan* (© Walt Disney Pictures)

39   © Treasure Island/Bridgeman Images

41   © Shutterstock

42   © Print Collector/Getty Images

44-47   © Shutterstock

49   © CSA-Printstock/iStockphoto

51   © Shutterstock

53   *Sir Henry Morgan and Chest of Treasure* (20th century), gouache on paper by Ron Embleton; Private Collection/© Look and Learn (Bridgeman Images)

54   *Men of the Jolly Roger* (20th century), gouache on paper by Ron Embleton; Private Collection/© Look and Learn (Bridgeman Images)

57   *Pacifying the South China Sea* (19th century); Hong Kong Maritime Museum (Bridgeman Images)

59   © Culture Club/Getty Images

60-75   © Shutterstock

76-79   © Culture Club/Getty Images

81   Library of Congress

82   © iStockphoto

85   © Marija Piliponyte, Shutterstock

86   © iStockphoto

89   From *Assassins Creed IV: Black Flag* (© Ubisoft)

91-93   © Shutterstock